I0190750

SLUGFEST
Magazine

Welcome fight fans to the first issue of Slugfest Magazine.

I have been a boxing fan since I was a little girl on my daddy's knee yelling at the television "kick his ass". Fighters are full of passion, heart, and determination. They are just looking for their place in this world. Many fighters are broken people rebuilding their lives one punch at a time. With each issue, I will bring you the passion, heart, and determination of the boxing world. I am determined and dedicated to win you over by bringing you the very best in boxing from around the world one issue at a time.

I am LaTavia Roberson, and this is Slugfest Magazine.

LaTavia

SLUGFEST
Magazine

CEO/ Reporter
LaTavia Roberson

Vice President / Reporter
Alfred Adams

Writers
Philip H. Anseimo
Dr. Matt Bucur
Jarrod Cash
Paul Hammontree

Vice President of Public Relations
Michael Lewis

Senior Editors
Susan Lungsford
Devon LaBonte
Johnny Walker

Head Photographer
Brandon Neal

Sponsership / Advertising
Randy Jackson

Graphic Designer
Jake Sparks

Copyright 2019

Slugfest Magazine is a imprint of
VIP Ink Publishing, L.L.C. Please feel
free to contact us at info@slugfestmagazine.com.

www.slugfestmagazine.com

f ⬤

Table of Contents

Mad Dog

Gene Hatcher Interview

By LaTavia Roberson and Devon LaBonte

Gene "Mad Dog" Hatcher's passion for boxing was first sparked at the age of ten, a passion that saw him become United States amateur champion and, after turning pro, world light welterweight champion. Throughout his career, Hatcher describes an intense battle with his spirituality, a battle that he says took hitting rock bottom in order to eventually "find the life he was meant to live." Today, Gene Hatcher runs Fitness 4:13, a self-defense gym in Aledo, Texas.

H atcher, looking back on his first encounter with boxing, describes his 10-year-old self as enthralled by the sport after attending a golden gloves competition with his father. He still recalls the passion that was ignited that day. "After watching the golden gloves, I told my dad 'I want to do that.' I was probably about the age of 10, and almost fifty-something years later, I've been through the boxing business, from the amateurs to the pros."

The former boxer goes on to elaborate on those aspects he found most challenging in his career. Revealing his toughest fight ever, Hatcher explains that it was "either Alfredo Escalera from Puerto Rico or Ubaldo Sacco from Argentina. Bumphus — winning the title from him — was a tough fight, but he just wasn't as physical as Escalera or Sacco. Those guys were in there to hurt somebody — you could tell. There's a difference — elbows, shoulders. Everything they can get away with, they get away with in the ring. And that's the type of fighter I am too."

When asked to share any words of wisdom for up-and-coming fighters, Hatcher said, "Just like I was taught in the boxing business — you make your fight in the gym or you leave your fight in the gym. You need to train as though you're going to win that fight. All the work should be done in the gym. When you get to the fight, your work should already be accomplished. You should be in the best shape that you can be in so that you can withstand what the fight may bring. Because each fight brings different things, more out of you than you ever imagine, some of them."

Reflecting on his career, Hatcher reveals a regret that, while competing, though he prepared mentally and physically for fights, he let his spirituality suffer. "The only thing that I've seen in the boxing business that I didn't accomplish when I was younger is — there's 100% physical, 100% mental and 100% spiritual, and if you can be 100% all the way then you've got a lot better chance of winning. Now, my spiritual part in my younger days wasn't like it needed to be and I learned from that. Today, I carry that with me and have a whole different life. But I think we need to go 100% in all three of them." He went on to further discuss the importance of this spirituality: "We all have a conscience. That conscience — if it's not clean and clear from the negatives, they fight against you. Fight against you working out every day, sparring every day. Negativity will hinder you from doing your best, if you're not 100% ready when you step in the ring."

The boxer appears to have mixed feelings about his world titles. While speaking with him, he initially describes them as "a great thing that anyone can accomplish." However, he also discusses at length the dark side of being a world champion, explaining how his career affected him spiritually and emotionally. "There is so much that goes along with a championship of the world that I would warn people about. It's not all its cracked up to be. There's winning, and then there's losing. When you're in the losing section of life, it's the hardest part of life. Losing my title drove me almost to shoot myself. My life had just ended, and I thought that all my friends and fans — you don't hear from people any more. Things change and you start allowing the negative choices, thoughts, to take over, but thanks to the Lord, who heard my cry and changed everything."

Hatcher credits this dark period and overcoming it as the biggest accomplishment of his life, explaining, "That's the only good thing about going to the bottom. It's an awful place. To ever get there and then to get through it, is the greatest thing I've ever done. The biggest accomplishment that has ever happened to me is that I found the real life that I was supposed to find — it just took me hell to find it. Maybe that's the best thing that can happen to somebody." Hatcher appears to have taken his spiritual epiphany to heart. In his business venture, 4:13 Fitness — and his preaching, which he does on the side — he explains he's now "just trying to help people."

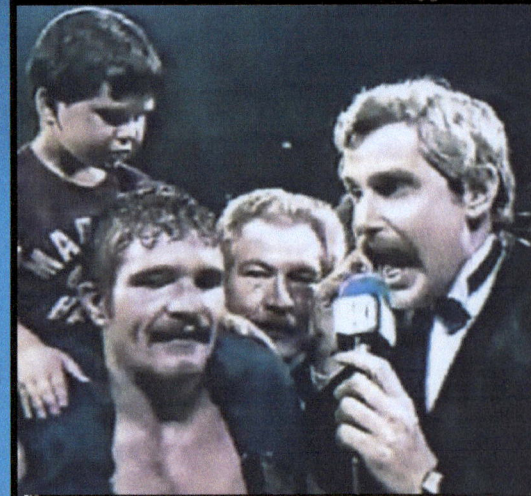

6

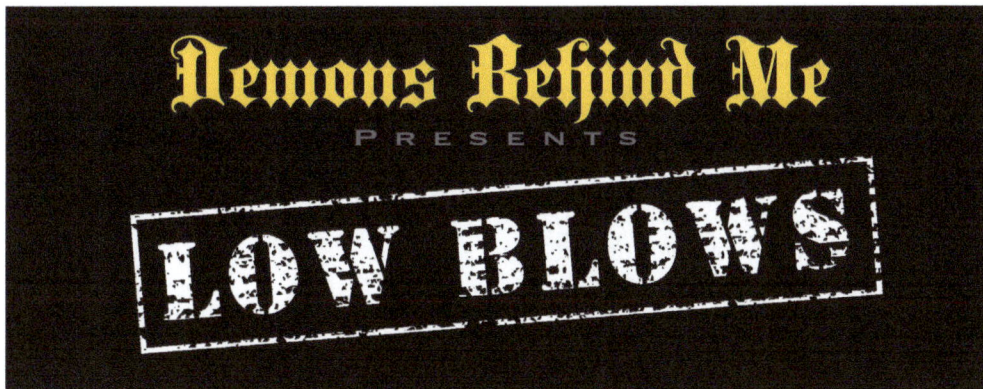

The Ronnie Dean Coleman Interview

By LaTavia Roberson and Devon LaBonte

Slugfest caught up with professional bodybuilder and eight-time Mr. Olympia champion Ronnie Dean Coleman to discuss the athlete's famed career.

Initially from Monroe, Louisiana, Coleman graduated from Grambling State University in 1984, having studied accounting. Finding himself unable to obtain a job in this field, he then became a police officer. At this point, Coleman's bodybuilding career was seemingly brought about by chance. On the recommendation of a friend, he attended Metroflex gym and met owner and amateur bodybuilder Brian Dobson, a meeting that would have a huge influence in Coleman's life. According to Coleman, Dobson repeatedly approached him with an offer — a free gym membership if he entered an upcoming competition. Coleman reflects on his early days in the industry, saying "I started competing because he gave me this free membership. I entered the first show and won, the second too. I won every show that I competed in for the first year and much of the second year, and that's how I got into bodybuilding."

After retiring in 2009, Coleman has since undergone 11 back surgeries due to injuries sustained over his long career as a bodybuilder and time spent playing college football. Though he is no longer able to train as a bodybuilder, Coleman maintains his positive outlook: "I have a really high pain tolerance so I've been able to deal with all the pain, and I've always been really focused on what it is I want to do. I just never let anything stop me. So, through all those surgeries, I went right back to the gym a couple months later, working out again and again and again." Despite undergoing three surgeries in 2018 alone, he insists "surgery has no limitations on me. I don't let anything stop me."

The former bodybuilder touched upon other struggles he endured while competing, explaining that as an African American man, he was faced with much opposition: "They tried to kick me out about halfway through, tried to change the score. It was a big-time struggle." Coleman's fight to become champion ended with him overcoming such adversity and winning, for a total of eight years, what is considered the world's ultimate bodybuilding competition. Coleman's modesty when discussing his titles becomes apparent: "A lot of people say I should have won nine. I disagree with them. I'm really happy I won eight, especially since I didn't think I would ever even win one."

In giving advice to a younger generation of hopeful athletes, Coleman emphasizes the impact that learning from others had on his career. He praises the efforts of his nutritionists and trainers, a team he says taught him all he needed to know to become champion. "I went from ninth place in Mr. Olympia to first place, and I tell people that was because of knowledge, because of what people taught me. I learned from others to get where I am." The athlete describes his younger life in detail, also accentuating the role sacrifice has played. "I made a ton of sacrifices, there were a lot of times I wanted to go to the movies, or to a game," he said. "I was stuck in the house eating the same food, a 24 hour, 7 day a week job. Everything was structured … The hardest thing I had to do was make those sacrifices, not go to parties, not go to clubs, not hang out with my friends, my girlfriend. I had to go to bed at a certain time every day, work out at the same time every day, do cardio at the same time every day."

When asked about the chance elements that brought about his transformation into world champion bodybuilder, Coleman insists that he initially "never intended to become a bodybuilder" and states, "Everybody has a purpose. Everybody has a calling. Try not to get your career and your calling mixed up. I didn't know the difference between the two until I won my first Mr. Olympia."

"Everyone wants to be a bodybuilder.But nobody wants to lift no heavy ass weights"
Ronnie Coleman

LOOKING AT THE FUTURE OF BOXING THROUGH THE HEAVYWEIGHT DIVISION
BY PHILIP H. ANSELMO

Photo by Danin Drahos

I love boxing, from amateurs to pros, small cards to pay-per-view events, and in all weight classes, yet I have no issue admitting I mainly follow the heavyweight division.

I can't help it.
It's how I roll.

I often hear the question, "Is the heavyweight division boring?" My rebuttal is often, "Or more to the point, is the heavyweight division boring in America?"

Well, I have some answers, but it requires a brief look back at the heavyweight division the world-over, and how things came to be.

Since 1885 to 1999— the USA had produced the vast majority of world heavyweight champions. I'm talking about undisputed, unified champions— champions recognized the world-over as, "The Man". And although the alphabet sanctioning body's titles are absolutely relevant in helping the linkage of champions, I'm focusing on a unified champ or a lineal champ.

In November of 1999, when Britain's Lennox Lewis defeated Evander Holyfield in their second fight by decision, the US's steely grip on the title was broken. Since Lewis's victory and subsequent unifying of the division's three top-regarded titles (at the time, the WBA, WBC & IBF), the drought of unified champions from the US has been glaring. Lewis had defended his title as World Champion (singular alphabet trinkets be damned) all over the globe, and was known, respected, feared and recognized as undisputed champ wherever he fought. Fans and pundits seemingly accepted this, as Lewis was extremely popular, even in the USA. And he'd beaten the man who beat "The Man".

Back then, HBO and Showtime were the main entities that showed the vast majority of world championship fights in the USA. Even ESPN, ESPN2's Friday Night Fights, USA Network's Tuesday Night Fights had significant cards televised. Tangible magazines still had a home on the shelves of stores, and each had their own rankings. However, it was The Ring magazine's rankings that were (and still are) seen as the pinnacle of actually following whom was the true champ.

Alas, when the great Lennox retired in January of 2004, this marked the end of a Golden Era of heavyweights for the majority of these same broadcasting companies, magazines, fans and pundits, especially in the US.

The rise of The Ukraine's Klitschko brothers had arrived, and in April of 2004, eldest brother Vitali knocked out Corrie Sanders in the 8th round to secure both the WBC trinket and World Champ status.

After Lewis retired, the aforementioned Ring Magazine had Vitali Klitschko rated #1 and Corrie Sanders rated #2 in their rankings. Of interest is that Sanders got his #2 rating by defeating the younger Klitschko brother, Wladimir.

Wladimir rebounded with a vengeance and went on to World Champion status after unifying the IBF, WBO and IBO laurels in 2009 after stopping Uzbekistan-born Ruslan Chagaev in nine rounds, whilst Vitali succumbed to injuries, forcing him into two different stints of retirements.

Despite Vitali coming back in 2008 to stop then-WBC Champ Sam Peter in eight rounds to regain the alphabet strap, younger brother Wladimir had cemented himself as World Champ by then whilst collecting the IBF, WBO and IBO laurels, thus it seemed there were two men atop the throne. Between the two, they held all the major belts, and cleared out the division's best contenders.

After Vitali retired for good in December of 2013, Wladimir reigned on as heavyweight champ until November of 2015, when the UK's Tyson Fury upset the odds and won a twelve round decision, thus breaking the Klitschko brother's reign as heavyweight kings.

I've reflected through this portion of heavyweight history for a specific reason—it was during this time, from 2004 till 2015—it seemed that boxing was indeed dying as a sport, once again, from an American viewpoint, at the very least. And as the old boxing adage proclaims, "As the heavyweights go, so does boxing".

Despite massive American television outlets showing many of the Klitschko brother's fights— HBO and Showtime, specifically—the brothers were deemed "boring" by these megacorporation's mouthpieces and nearly all American media.

In truth, it was sociopathically insincere for anyone to proclaim either Klitschko brother "boring". Wladimir's final record was 64-5, 54 KO's and Vitali's was 45-2, 41 KO's. Hardly records that scream, "boring". The brothers often filled 60,000 seat arenas in Germany, but did nowhere near that kind of business in America.

There was, without a doubt, an anti-Klitschko brother sentiment rife within the American media during their careers, and it all stemmed from the fact that America hadn't produced a globally recognized world champion since George Foreman knocked out Michael Moorer in 1994.

Sure, Americans won versions of the alphabet titles between November 1994 and November 1999, but it was Britain's Lennox Lewis who eventually became unified World Champ in 1999, defeating the superb Evander Holyfield in their second meeting for the unified world title.

Looking at the modern heavyweight landscape, there are factors as to why there's not a unified, crowned heavyweight champion, yet there's plenty of reason for boxing fans to be excited moving forward, including American fans.

In December 2013, after Vitali Klitschko retired for good, the WBC title became vacant. In May 2014, Canada's Bermaine Stiverne (by way of Haiti) defeated American Chris Arreola for the vacant title, but lost it in early 2015 by unanimous decision to American Deontay Wilder. Wilder later knocked Stiverne out in less than a round in a rematch.

In the current year, 2019, Wilder is still WBC heavyweight champ. And with a record of 40-0-1, 39 KO's, the 6-7"-220 lb. Wilder is easily one of the top three heavyweights on the planet. And he's definitely one of the top two punchers in the world today. Deontay is currently scheduled to face lineal World Champ, Tyson Fury, 27-0-1, 19 KO's, in a rematch of last December's excellent scrap that ended in draw. Fury out-boxed Wilder for most of the fight, but Wilder's brutal power dropped the 6-9" Fury twice.

In 2015, Fury defeated Wladimir Klitschko for the lineal heavyweight championship and the alphabet laurels that come with being a unified World Champ. However, the big "Gypsy King" relinquished all the alphabet titles during a tumultuous year-and-a-half away from the sport, but is still recognized today by boxing purists as the lineal champ. The fact Fury came back and fought Deontay Wilder to a draw last year after only two comeback fights shows how talented he is. Having Fury in the modern day mix is tremendous for the sport. Plus, as lineal champ, he potentially gets to reclaim his World Champion status against today's best.

Perhaps the biggest name to emerge out of heavyweight modernity is Britain's Anthony Joshua, 22-0, 21 KO's. At 6-6"-250 lbs., Joshua is pegged by most experts as the most talented of the modern lot. He certainly looks the part, but time and fights against Fury and Wilder will tell a lot more about the Olympic Gold-winning pugilist.

Joshua became IBF champ after Tyson Fury's brief retirement in April of 2016, knocking then-champ Charles Martin out in less than two-rounds. Then, in April of 2017, in an almost-passing-of-the-torch, Joshua stopped former World Champ Wladimir Klitschko in the eleventh round for the vacant "WBA Super Champion" trinket.

This would have been a true passing-of-the-guard had Tyson Fury not defeated Klitschko for the World title first.

In March of 2018, Joshua defeated Joseph Parker for his WBO belt. Parker was undefeated going into this contest, but Joshua's pressure was too much. Joshua has unified three of the four major titles, all once held by Tyson Fury and never lost in the ring, and captured the hearts of Great Britain's boxing fans. He sells out huge venues there every time he fights, with attendances upward to 80,000 paying to watch him hone his craft.

With the exception of perhaps Tyson Fury, Joshua is the "A-Side" fighter, no matter who he faces. And for the up-and-coming contender, landing a fight with Joshua is akin to finding the treasure at the end of a rainbow of left hooks.

So, to recap, heading into 2019 we have Anthony Joshua, the WBO, IBF, and WBA "Super Champion", Deontay Wilder, the WBC champ, and Tyson Fury, the lineal heavyweight champion, all fighting for supremacy in the glamour division. Looks excellent to my eyes. And these potential scenarios should look tantalizing to any sane boxing fan.

With Fury and Wilder set for their rematch, the winner must face Anthony Joshua to settle who is the best heavyweight on the planet and World Champion heading into 2020.
It's a must.

At this time of writing, Joshua is very close to coming to terms for a fight with huge American, Jarrell "Big Baby" Miller, 23-0-1, 20 KO's. At 300+ lbs., Miller holds the weight well, and is 6-4". This would mark Joshua's first trek to America to fight as a pro. He's likeable and marketable, and if he gets past Miller, Joshua will leave an impact in the USA. A fight with Deontay Wilder in the near future is highly anticipated.

This is must-watch action, especially if it all pans out and the best eventually fight the best. Joshua, Fury and Wilder are considered the top names heading into 2019 and beyond, but there are contenders beneath them in the ratings/rankings worthy of note—

Britain's Dillian Whyte, 25-1, 19 KO's, whose lone loss came to Anthony Joshua before he was champ, has improved greatly since, and with every outing. He's an action fighter, he fights often, and some would argue the most deserving of a shot at any of the top three. Kubrat Pulev, 26-1, 13 KO's, of Bulgaria is still highly rated and coming off a victory over Hughie Fury. His lone loss was to the great Wladimir Klitschko. Luis Ortiz, 30-1-2NC, 26 KO's, is a US fighter by way of Cuba, and a dangerous southpaw, despite getting on with age. His lone loss was to Deontay Wilder in a good back-and-forth scrap. New Zealand's Joseph Parker, 25-2, 19 KO's, is still around and looking to get his career back on track, as is Russia's Alexander Povetkin, 34-2, 24 KO's. Both Parker and Povetkin are dangerous opponents, especially for up-and-comers.

Veterans like Germany's Christian Hammer, 24-5, 14 KO's, Finland's Robert Helenius, 28-2, 16 KO's, and Australia's Lucas Browne, 27-1, 24 KO's, are fighting on to get a crack at one of the top three, but there's a new wave of contenders on the rise, and the aforementioned are gatekeepers at this point in their respective careers.

America's Jarrell Miller, Dominic Breazeale, 20-1, 18 KO's, Adam Kownacki (by way of Poland), 19-0, 15 KO's, and Michael Hunter, 16-1, 11 KO's, are in the hunt, climbing the ratings and are as tough as nails. Canada's (by way of Columbia) Oscar Rivas, 26-0, 18 KO's is coming off his biggest victory over durable Bryant Jennings, Sergey Kuzmin, 14-0-1, 11 KO's, of Russia keeps winning, and Germany's Agit Kabayel, 18-0, 12 KO's is rated by three of the four major sanctioning bodies—all guys to watch out for.

And then there's another layer of young boxers on the rise to keep an eye on—

Croatia's Filip Hrgovic, 7-0, 5 KO's, looks like the second coming of Vitali Klitschko, Germany's Tom Schwarz, 23-0, 16 KO's, looks like a young Andrew Golata—the one that boxed circles around Riddick Bowe—and Britain's Joe Joyce, 7-0, 7 KO's has shown plenty of promise and power. These are names to remember moving forward into 2020 and beyond.

Other cats worthy of note are Britain's Nathan Gorman, 15-0, 10 KO's and Daniel Dubois, 9-0, 8 KO's, Croatia's Petar Milas, 13-0, 10 KO's, Canadian (by way of the Ukraine) Oleksandr Teslenko, 15-0, 12 KO's, Russia's Rostislav Plechko, 13-0, 13 KO's, the USA's Tyrone Spong, 13-0, 12 KO's and Darmani Rock, 14-0, 9 KO's, Kazakhstan's Ivan Dychko, 7-0, 7 KO's, Russian by way of Canada, Arslanbek Makhmudov, 6-0, 6 KO's, Nigeria's Efe Ajagba, 8-0, 7 KO's, the Ukraine's Vladyslav Sirenko, 10-0, 9 KO's and Oleksandr Zakhozhyi, 10-0, 8 KO's, and Denmark's Kem Ljungquist, 7-0, 5 KO's.

And don't even get me started on unified cruiserweight champ Oleksandr Usyk moving up to heavyweight!
You KNOW I love it!

Make no mistake, these are very exciting times to look forward to in the heavyweight division! And as the olde saying goes—"As the heavyweights go, so does boxing".
Indeed.
-Philip H. Anselmo 2019

> "In boxing, it is about the obsession of getting the most from yourself: wanting to dominate the world like a hungry young lion."
> Anthony Joshua

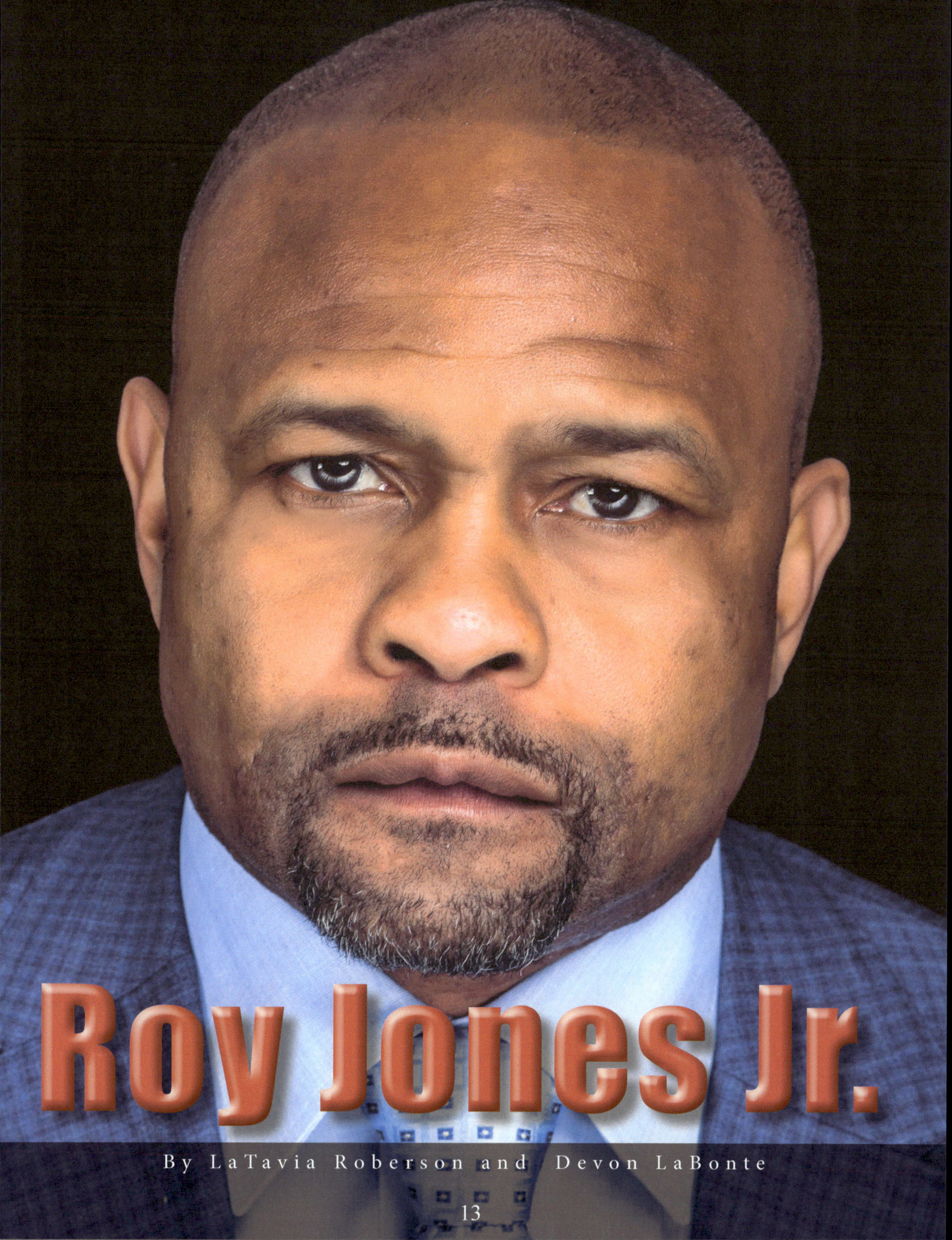

Roy Jones Jr.

By LaTavia Roberson and Devon LaBonte

Roy Jones Jr. weighs in on his legendary career in an in-depth interview, from that controversial 1998 Olympics decision to his approach to training upcoming fighters. The Florida native's career is considered to be one of the most prolific in boxing history. Turning professional in 1989 and competing in a total of 75 pro fights, Jones goes down in history as a multiple title winner across four weight classes and the first boxer to start his career as a junior middleweight and go on to win a heavyweight title.

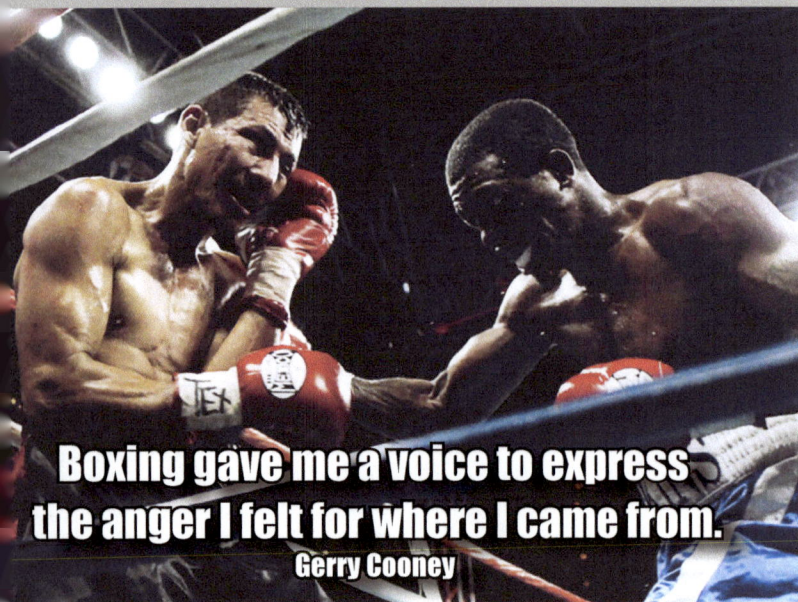

Boxing gave me a voice to express the anger I felt for where I came from.
Gerry Cooney

Describing himself as a "natural agitator," the athlete recalls his early experiences with the sport: "When I was a kid, my father used to watch Muhammad Ali. I think I was about five years old, and my father was watching Muhammad Ali and Joe Frazier. When you're that young, you want to do anything that will pique your father's interest, and that had my father's interest. So I started watching it. What I was seeing was one guy outthinking the other guy, making this other guy mad, using his negative energy against him, and being an agitator. Because I saw myself as a natural agitator already, I thought, if somebody could teach me how to use my hands, then I could do this too. That's when my passion for it started. Right then, I knew boxing was a sport that I can do."

The boxer remembers his first championship win as the moment he finally felt the significance of his accomplishments. "My first world title win made me feel like I had accomplished something I had wanted to do since I was a kid. My first dream was to go to the Olympics, but they robbed me of my gold medal. My next dream was to be world champion. That was my next goal, so when I finally won, it was almost a relief and weight off my shoulders. He further describes the experience: "the first belt was me solidifying that I was meant to be a boxer

When asked about his toughest fight in the ring, Jones details his first fight against Tarver: "I lost weight from heavyweight all the way back down to light heavyweight. So for 25 lbs. of muscle being lost, totally dehydrated, only working off of the strength of my heart, and still, to win it—that was the first time I had to show that person, pull out that guy with the heart of a champion. It was the first time in my life when people saw me when the chips were down, and I had to persevere a little comeback. A lot of people told me that they loved me as a champion before this fight, but this fight taught them who I really am."

As Jones reflects on his career, he reveals how he may have done things differently. He discusses the impact of his choice to delay retirement. "I would only change one thing about my career. When I came back and beat Tarver, I knew that was my last goal. Looking back, when you don't have any goals any more, then you should stop. My goal was to become heavyweight champ and come back and recapture my light heavyweight championship. After that, I let the warrior in me get in front of everything else."

The boxer touched upon the controversial and hotly contested decision that robbed him of the gold at the 1988 Seoul Olympics: 'The outcome of that fight led to the demise of Olympic boxing. It used to be dominated by the U.S., but not any more. That decision lowered the integrity of the situation. By not fixing that, it makes it seems like it's ok for people to be treated like that. The Eastern European world picked it up. We're not as prominent as we used to be. They're dominating the Olympics now. The thing is that usually whoever dominates the Olympics is who dominates the pro game years later."

The athlete also commented on the personal ramifications of the loss. He credits the experience as an "example of God showing you the worst thing you think can happen in life, and proving it to be the best thing that can happen to you in life. Most of the people I work with now are overseas people. And these people know me from not only what happened to me in the Olympics, but how I reacted to it. That made them want to know who this 19 –year-old kid was and so that was a blessing in disguise the whole time."

Jones revealed that, as a professional boxer, the hardest fight is sometimes outside the ring. "The hardest fight is staying positive-minded, staying focused when people say you can't. Because when I signed the fight for heavyweight championship of the world, so many people that I don't even hear from told me I couldn't do it. How are you going to tell me differently from what God tells me to go do? I hear them, but I don't hear them because I already have confirmation from the man above that this is what I need to do. The hardest thing is being able to deal with the constant negativity and still go forward with a positive attitude. When people say negative things, you want to retaliate. But it's not about retaliation. You retaliate with actions. That's the best retaliation, showing people that you can do what they say you can't."

Jones, also well-known as a rapper and actor, when asked about any effect his other ventures may have had on his boxing career, states: "I love boxing, and nothing that I ventured into took away from my boxing. If anything, those things may have enhanced my boxing. Basketball, and to a certain degree the rapping enhanced my boxing. Acting, movies—whatever I'm doing—only enhanced my career."

In discussing how his other endeavors impacted him, Jones says, "You have a whole other view of how people look at you and what you're doing and what you stand for. It made me pay more attention to who I really was and what I was doing."

Offering a rare glimpse of the man outside the sport, Jones also discusses his day-to-day lifestyle. On food preferences, he comments: "I'm a seafood man more so than anything else. I love chicken, but if you ask me today what I want, that would be seafood. Lobster is my favorite." Though the boxer avoids watching television aside from sports, he does reveal himself to be a fan of kung fu movies. Jones also discussed the role that animals play in his daily life, and, commenting on this, states, "I love animals. I love raising them. They teach you about life."

Currently, Jones promotes and trains fighters, as well as occasionally commentating. "I'm still training fighters now, and I promote. I have my promotional company. I love training fighters. I love passing down what I've learned from boxing, what I've learned from life. I love passing it down to the young guy. A lot of the young guys that come up have talent but don't know where to go. A lot of the guys are lost—some need help, some need a little encouragement."

Jones, on his approach to training, says 'I'm not just training a fighter. I'm training a person. I strive to make them not only better fighters, but better young men."

The boxer, describing what the future holds, talks about his latest business venture in Russia. "I'm trying to open some gyms in Russia. I have a group of guys opening up some gyms in Russia at the moment. Because, like I said, domination at the Olympics usually leads to domination of the professionals. Because the guys in the Russian area are the ones dominating the Olympics, it's smart that I have a head start getting these guys, because they'll be the guys of tomorrow who will be dominating professional boxing."

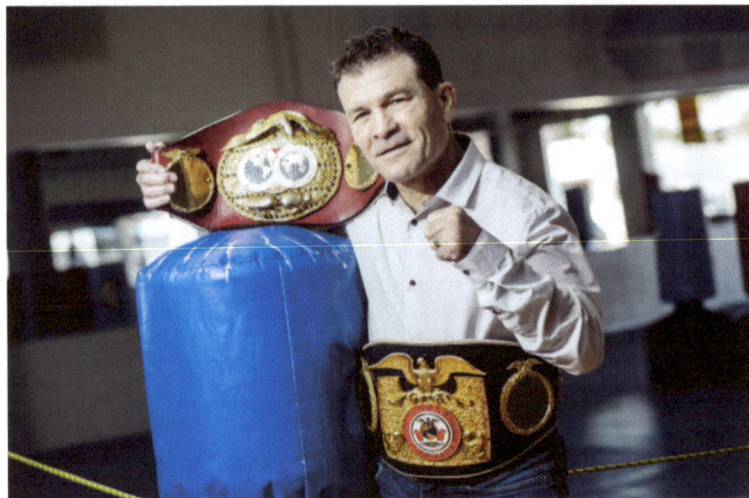

Troy Dorsey Interview
By LaTavia Roberson Devon LaBonte

Troy Dorsey, first man ever to hold world titles in both boxing and kickboxing, talks us through how he got his start in self-defense and the journey that led him to his titles. Dorsey, now retired, runs a successful karate school in Mansfield, Texas — now teaching martial arts just across the street from where he first started karate back in 1974. The athlete recalls how this early start in karate led him down the path to becoming a world champion multiple times over.

What got you into in self-defense?

I was getting bullied at school. I was in the fifth grade and small for my age, and I came home crying one day. My dad, who owned a gas station in downtown Mansfield, took my two brothers and I to a karate school here in Mansfield. And now, I'm located right across the street from where I started karate in 1974.

Initially, what made you choose kickboxing as a career?

I started fighting in these karate tournaments — what's called point karate — so its not continuous fighting. You fight for two minutes, and if someone scores, they stop the match. They call for points. I believe kickboxing began in '75 or '76, and in 1979, I went to some kickboxing matches that were in Dallas, and — American kickboxing is where you wear boxing gloves and you're allowed to kick, and everything is above the belt. So I went

to watch some fights in Dallas, and I thought, "I've got to do this". Two months later, I fought in my first kickboxing match in October 1979. I was hooked.

Then, fast-forward to 1983. My instructor and I had a disagreement, plus I wanted to become a better kickboxer, so I needed to learn more about boxing. So I went to the boxing gym, and I saw Stevie Cruz. He was there, and later became a world champion, and I was his sparring partner. Sometimes, people think sparring partners are used just as — what you might say — as meat. But me, I was sparring partner for Stevie Cruz, and they may have been using me that way. But then, he won the world title. He was a big underdog, and he beat Barry McGuigan. When he won that fight and I was working with him, I thought, "I think I can do this too". So I started boxing.

Toughest fight ever?

I had 68 fights — 33 pro boxing matches and 35 kickboxing matches. There were some really tough fights, but I think the toughest one, physically, emotionally, and in any other way, was against Jesse James Leija. He and I are friends now. We just texted last night. Every once in a while, we reach out to each other. He's just a great guy.

I do want to talk to you about your surgery.

In June 1994, I fought Oscar De La Hoya, and I got cut in the first round so between the first and second round, they looked at the cut and the doctor stopped the fight. I jumped up off the stool. I was so mad. I thought they were stopping it because De La Hoya was the golden boy and I was the first world champion that he fought. Maybe I was his sixth or eighth fight, I don't remember.

With De La Hoya, I was cut, and I was fighting. The way the cut was, it was so deep and long. The blood was going down the side of my face, but I could see. The doctor in Las Vegas was stitching me up — it was a two-inch gash — and he said that there's a surgery I could get because I had these calcium deposits. So I had this surgery where they made an incision. They cut me across the forehead, like the place where you wear headphones, all the way across. They pulled my forehead down, the skin to the edge of my eyes, and shaved the bones. Then, they cut out some of my eyelid because the extra skin can cause cutting also — you're more likely to get cut.

So I had that surgery and then I fought again in '95, '96, '97. I won a world title in boxing and a couple world titles in kickboxing during that time. And in 1998, I fought in the Alamodome in San Antonio, and I got cut. I don't remember what round it was, and they stopped the fight in the seventh or eighth round. I was 35 then. I put my wife and my parents through h-e-l-l — them seeing me get cut and bleed and get busted up. And I was 35 years old so I thought it was the time to retire.

But I've been doing martial arts since '74. I opened my first school in '81, and then I opened this school in '99. I would continue to teach and train during some of that time. My wife would run the school for me. When you're fighting those big fights, those world title fights, you can't just train two days a week. I'd train 6 days a week, taking one day off.

I had my wife run the school so that everything was just taken care of so I didn't have to be there.

For aspiring fighters, what kind of inspiration would you give to them?

It's a huge commitment just like anything else. You have to commit. It took a lot of hard work, dedication and support: my parents' support, my wife's support. I had a great team. My manager, my parents and my trainer — I had a lot of great support. It's not just me. I won the world titles. I got the credit, and I got the belts. But there were a lot of people behind me, especially my wife and my trainers who help me get prepared. My wife — she had to do a lot of work. She made sacrifices for me that not many wives I believe would have made.

Paulie Ayala

By LaTavia Roberson Devon LaBonte

Paulie Ayala is best known for his two world title wins, having held the WBA bantamweight and the IBO super bantamweight titles. Following his retirement, Ayala founded Punching Out Parkinson's, teaching a program in his gym in Fort Worth, Texas of non-contact boxing techniques designed to help those suffering from loss of coordination and strength due to the degenerative disease. We had a chance to sit down with the two-time world champion, looking back on his career and involvement in the sport which spans over 25 years

What got you interested in boxing?

I started doing exhibitions when I was four years old. My father was a Vietnam vet — so coming out of Vietnam in the 70s when I was born — I was raised to be like a Marine, a Devil Dog. It was a pretty hardcore upbringing … My older brother boxed a bit, and they started me at 4 years old, putting me in exhibitions.

How did you feel when you won your first title?

For me, winning that first world title — when they said those words and I knew — chills came down my body because I remember saying that when I was a little kid. It was the same as when I daydreamed and imagined it. It was surreal. I couldn't believe it was happening, but it was real. What made it even sweeter is that the guy I beat had been undefeated for 10 years.

I was just about to ask you about your biggest slugfest.

It was that guy. His name was Johnny Tapia, and his ring name was Mi Vida Loca, meaning "my crazy life". To go in and beat him—I was the first guy that ever beat him. What was good too was that his trainer was Freddie Roach who has trained Manny Pacquiao. People think that he became Freddie Roach after he got Pacquiao, but he was Freddie back then too—just nobody knew him as much as they know him now. So, at the time, I felt like I beat Johnny and Freddie.

If you were still boxing today, what would you do differently? And what would you advise your old self to do differently?

There was a point in my career when I was trying to get the best fights against some of the best guys, and I had to move up in weight. I was then the world champion in junior featherweight and I had an opportunity to move up to featherweight to fight for a world title against Érik Morales who's a multiple world champion. He's in the hall of fame. The way I did move up — I think sports science was not as evolved as it is today so the ways that I trained back then would have been different.

In what ways?

It's more specific sport training as far as strength training and conditioning outside of the boxing. I think it was time for me to change my campsites, maybe to change people on my team. I loved my trainers, but, to me, I think their age was catching up with them at the time…but in hindsight I think that everything that went, it went according to plan, and winning two world titles in two weight divisions was something that I never thought would happen.

In 1999, I got "Fighter of the Year", and that's when everyone –Mayweather, Pacquiao, De La Hoya, Vargas, Tyson, Holyfield, Roy Jones were all still fighting in '99. I got Ring Magazine's "Fighter of the Year" and that gave me a feeling like I really belong here, no matter what else happens after this. It's already in ink, written in the books. So whatever else happens, that's just icing on the cake. It was a big accomplishment because they just pick one guy.

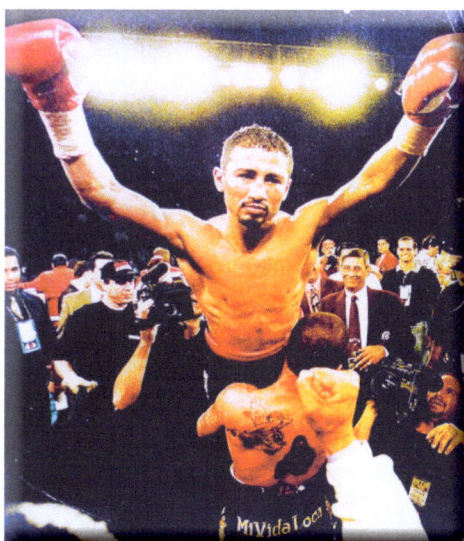

As a boxer and now a trainer, what do you look for in young and upcoming fighters?

Of course, he has to be athletic, have killer instinct, has to have heart, but most of all he has to be smart, a smart guy that knows how to think and figure out problems. That's really what fighting is. You have to figure out how to fight. We could write out a plan, but it's always going to change. I tell my guys, my fighters that I have now, you're not going to be the biggest punch, not going to be the fastest guy, might not even be the toughest guy or best fighter. But if you're smarter than them on the night — that's what you need to be. I wasn't knocking out everybody, so I had to figure out how I was going to win. These guys, a lot of them had more knockouts than I had fights so I had to figure it all out.

Slugfest Pick of the Week: Garcia v Spence

On March 16th in AT&T Stadium in Dallas, Texas two of the biggest fighters in the boxing world will clash when Mikey Garcia (39-0-0) takes on Errol Spence Jr. (24-0-0) in a fight where history will be on the line: Mikey will look to become a five weight world champion. The last man to achieve this goal was Floyd Mayweather in 2014.

A pro since 2006 Garcia has held world titles at featherweight, super featherweight, lightweight, and super lightweight. The 31 year old now will now focus his talent on welterweight champion Errol Spence Jr. Although Mikey does have 30 of his wins by knockout, it's his slick fundamentals and punch placement that have given Mikey his best performances. Garcia is no stranger to a move up in weight class as he has chose to move up in weight multiple times since his layoff between 2014 and 2016. That layoff came from his long drawn out court battle with his former promoter Top Rank. Now being represented by UK based promoter Eddie Hearn. In his last three fights Mikey has rattled off three unanimous decision wins over the likes of Robert Easter Jr. (21-1-0), Sergey Lipinets (14-1-0), and Adrien Broner. In all of them, he was able to use his superior fundamentals to control his larger opponents. Now facing Spence he will need to use those same qualities to attempt to get the win. His punch placement and pace is going to be a major factor in this fight and may be the ultimate decider.

Errol Spence Jr. will be making his fourth defense of the IBF title he has held since May 2017. He has also stopped eleven straight opponents in a streak dating back to September 2014. Boasting a record of 24-0 with 21 KO's, he has power to go along with his boxing skills. Spence turned pro after his appearance in the Olympics in 2012. To win this fight, he will need to use his greatest advantage: his size. Some say he is large even for the 147lb class, using his fight against Kell Brook as an example. It is possible that Spence could eventually move up to light-middle later n his career.

Jarrod's Pick:
I strongly feel that the 2 weight jump will play out like many others we've seen in the past, with the larger fighter ultimately prevailing. Garcia has a chance, working in close, slipping punches and countering, but despite his great skills, I think he falls to Spence by 7th rd TKO

Paul's pick:
In my opinion this fight in ultimately going to come down to the size and punching power of Spence. Also, his trend of picking up the punching pace in times of adversity as well as the later rounds. Although Mikey Garcia is the better fundamental boxer Spence tends to also use his fundamentals to fire off great body shots. Those body shots will ultimately be Garcia's undoing in the end. Errol Spence by KO round 8.

Jarrod Cash is a former Golden Gloves boxer who now trains in mixed martial arts. Paul Hammontree is former amateur wrester who also now trains in MMA. Both of the guys live in the Fight Capitol of the World, Las Vegas, and are lifelong fans of not just boxing but all Combat Sports. They are hosts of the show Smokin' Weed And Talkin' MMA (S.W.A.T. MMA) which can be heard on Thursday nights 8pm Central on WBUZ95 on radio. net or the Orange Radio app, as well as found on iTunes, Google Play, YouTube and more. Find out more at
http://www.swatmma.com

Are You Eating to Win?
Dr. Matt Bucur

Weeks and months of training. Countless hours in the gym everyday, giving it your all and leaving nothing on the table. You've put in the work, dropped the weight needed to make your class, and prepared yourself mentally to win. There is nothing more that can be or could have been done, right? Wrong.

This happens time and time again and I've seen it with athletes in every sport. Boxing being the one area where the athlete does everything I've mentioned above, only to be left lying on the mat after being knocked out 2 rounds in. What happened? Did he train incorrectly? Was he not mentally prepared? Where was the strength and energy he had the weeks leading up to the big day? My answer to this very real scenario is…nutrition.

Nutrition is the one area where bodybuilders have learned to manipulate and use nutrition to their advantage in order to achieve their physique and strength goals. This is also the one area many athletes are beginning to realize can and will give them an advantage over their competition. Food is the body's source of fuel. As athletes our bodies are put through some of the most rigorous training any human will endure. Muscle is constantly being broken down and repaired; trained to perform and expend energy in precise ways in order to make a certain move, lift a certain weight or endure long periods of stress. Food provides the building blocks your muscles utilize to come back bigger, stronger and faster. Without proper nutrition, you will NEVER be performing at your highest potential. There is no amount of training, no nutritional supplement or no amount of willpower that can overcome a poor diet. The same way a Ferrari needs premium gasoline in order to run at optimal speeds, the same way your body will never run, lift or fight at its highest potential without proper nutrition.

So what is proper nutrition? When I structure nutrition plans for my athletes, I focus on the 3 main macronutrients from which all calories are derived from. Protein, Carbs, and Fats. Maybe we are looking to pack on as much muscle as possible. Or drop weight and fat while maintaining the strength, energy and agility we trained so hard for. I always attack nutrition the same way, with the same concepts.

Protein. The granddaddy macro you always hear about in the gym. Protein always comes first. Eating enough protein will ensure your muscle are receiving adequate amino acids in order to repair and restructure themselves bigger and stronger than before you trained. Depending on our immediate goals, I like to focus on 1 to 1.5 grams per pound of bodyweight.

Next is carbohydrates. Carbs are the one area we can manipulate the most depending on the athlete's genetics, build structure and current goals. The main focus here will be to eat enough to fuel the body for optimal performance, but not too much to where we're packing on unneeded weight through fat accumulation. The types of carbs are important as well. By prioritizing whole grains and complex carbohydrates, we can keep blood sugars level, along with providing the body with the essential fiber and micronutrients needed to maintain overall health.

Last but not least is our fat intake. Although we normally keep this on the lower end (unless we follow a Keto or carb cycling diet) healthy fats are vital for optimal hormone production, brain function, cardiovascular health and overall satiety. The total fat intake will be highly dependent on the amount of carbs we are consuming and the type of diet we're following.

Nutrition is not rocket science but it is a science. Do not leave it to chance and hope that burger and fries is "good enough" to help you recover and win. It just wont work. I've been in the fitness industry for over 15 years and have helped athletes across all sports and all ages not only look and feel their best, but perform their best come game day. If you want to perform at your absolute best and display everything that you've trained for years to achieve, do not make the mistake that so many athletes make by avoiding proper nutrition. By dialing in your exact macro needs and having a coach lay the ground work, there is no goal you cannot achieve, within your genetic limits of course. And if you only have one takeaway from this article its this: Feed the muscle. Burn the fat.

*Dr. Matt Bucur holds a Doctorate degree in pharmacy and is an IFBB Professional athlete in Men's Physique. He is the Co-Founder and CEO at MDRN Athlete, LLC, providing elite training and nutrition programs online along with the sports industry's newest and cleanest performance supplements. Find out more at www.mdrnathlete.com

The Underground

Presents

Darrick Stewart

by Alfred Adams and Devon LaBonte

"Instead of me being a product of my surroundings, I started looking at how I can utilize my surroundings to make things better."

Darrick Stewart

Stewart mentions Cooper as somebody "that's made a big impact with the gym, with his relationship with Roy Jones Jr.—those two have a great brotherhood. Cooper is really great at relating to the kids, being a mentor, not just a trainer."

Stewart highlights some of the promising fighters training with Uppercuts Gym. Ariele Davis, one of the nation's elite amateur boxers, according to Stewart, is "going to be one of the top female fighters out there. We're in the process of supporting her amateur career, but also letting her know how important it is to take advantage of the pro opportunities that are out there. She is very talented and will be a great pro. She has a great personality and spirit—she's very grounded. Alexis Martin, another upcoming fighter at the gym, also has the potential to be a great pro—she's very aggressive. She's in the process of honing her skills, and with the support and foundations we're building for them, in the next couple months to a year, they will be great fighters." Stewart also remarks on expanding the gym's management opportunities: "We do have fighters and are letting them know the opportunities that are out there. We're reaching out to a couple of pro fighters to say that we are in the process of being able to support them through management."

Commenting on the gym's involvement in the community, including its after school enrichment program and charity drives, Stewart emphasizes the family aspect of the business, saying "We call it the Uppercuts 'family.' If you make it too business-oriented, you can go over a lot of people's heads who need your help."

Darrick Stewart discusses his passion for boxing and entrepreneurial spirit that led him to open Uppercuts Boxing Gym in New Orleans, LA. After graduating with a bachelor's in computer science and working as a regional tech manager, Stewart recalls that his passion for boxing led him to change career paths, eventually opening his own gym. Describing his personal connection to boxing, Stewart states: "With the boxing, that's something I was very passionate about. When I was about 10 years old, my dad bought me boxing gloves. I liked the competitive nature of boxing. Boxing builds self-esteem, improving your internal and external self. Boxing is sort of like redemption—it gives people opportunity throughout all walks of life. Learning how to box and getting yourself in shape builds self-esteem and discipline. Instead of me being a product of my surroundings, I started looking at how I can utilize my surroundings to make things better."

March 2019 marks the fifth anniversary of the gym's opening. Stewart insists that with each year comes new insight into his business: "Each year I learn something different that I can do with the business, different avenues and angles I can take." He describes how the gym has evolved, dealing with nonprofits, schools, and increasingly focusing on contributing to the community. Uppercuts Gym's head trainer, Valrice Cooper, the "Cornerman," is possibly best known for training Roy Jones Jr.

Stewart touches on the gym's future, sharing that the most significant goal would be to establish the gym as a nonprofit, and to secure funding to further give back to the community saying, "We have provided a lot of support throughout the years in the community. It would be great to get funding that's needed to take the program to the next level, for traveling and sponsorship for events, so we can help the kids— help them with clothes and supplies. We recently did a school drive and were able to give school supplies to over 300 children." Stewart's vision of the gym's future puts the focus on supporting his community.

26

www.ingramcontent.com/pod-product-compliance
Lightning Source LLC
Chambersburg PA
CBHW041239020426
42331CB00002B/5